A TRUE BOOK™

Why It Matters

The Bill of Rights

Ruth Bjorklund

Children's Press®
An Imprint of Scholastic Inc.

Content Consultant
Kerry Sautner
Chief Learning Officer
National Constitution Center
Philadelphia, Pennsylvania

We thank the staff of the National Constitution Center in
Philadelphia, Pennsylvania, for their help with this book.

We also thank Deimosa Webber-Bey for her insight into Native American history.

Teacher Adviser
Rachel Hsieh

Library of Congress Cataloging-in-Publication Data
Title: The Bill of Rights : why it matters to you / Ruth Bjorklund.
Description: New York : Children's Press®, an imprint of Scholastic, Inc., 2019. | Series: A true book |
    Includes bibliographical references and index.
Identifiers: LCCN 2019007686 | ISBN 9780531231814 (library binding : alk. paper) | ISBN
    9780531239933 (pbk. : alk. paper)
Subjects: LCSH: United States. Constitution. 1st-10th Amendments—Juvenile literature. |
    Constitutional amendments—United States—Juvenile literature. | Civil rights—United States—
    Juvenile literature.
Classification: LCC KF4750 .B553 2019 | DDC 342.7308—dc23
LC record available at https://lccn.loc.gov/2019007686

SCHOLASTIC, CHILDREN'S PRESS, A TRUE BOOK™, and associated logos are trademarks and/or
registered trademarks of Scholastic Inc.

Scholastic Inc., 557 Broadway, New York, NY 10012

1 2 3 4 5 6 7 8 9 10 R 29 28 27 26 25 24 23 22 21 20

**Front cover: A copy of the Bill
of Rights on the U.S. flag**

**Back cover: A demonstration in
Washington, D.C., in 2018**

Find the Truth!

Everything you are about to read is true *except* for one of the sentences on this page.

Which one is **TRUE**?

T or F   Connecticut was the first state to approve the Bill of Rights.

T or F   The Bill of Rights allows you to voice your beliefs by playing music.

Find the answers in this book.

Contents

The Miranda rights are named after Ernesto Miranda.

The **BIG** Truth

Should the First Amendment Change?

4

A mural celebrating the importance of voting

Young soldiers

Think About It!

Take a look at this photo. Thousands of people are gathered near the U.S. Capitol. Is it a parade? Or maybe it is something else? Why do you think the crowd chose to be in Washington, D.C.? Do you think what they are doing will make a difference? What does it have to do with the Bill of Rights?

Intrigued?
Want to know more? Turn the page!

Congressperson Ayanna Pressley of Massachusetts encourages citizens to stand up for their beliefs.

If you think the people are marching to defend a cause they believe in, you are right! Usually people gather in demonstrations to voice their political, economic, or social points of view. People who planned this march believed the best place to speak out would be in the nation's capital. They wanted to be sure their lawmakers and president listened to them.

Protests like this can happen thanks to the Bill of Rights. This is a set of 10 **amendments**, or changes, to the U.S. Constitution. It was written more than two centuries ago to protect many basic rights. Without it, people might have to keep political meetings secret. Those brave enough to protest could be thrown in jail without a trial.

A family views one of the remaining handwritten copies of the Constitution and Bill of Rights in Washington, D.C.

It took the *Mayflower*
66 days to sail from
England to the Americas.

NORTH
AMERICA

Plymouth
England

Plymouth
Colony

Cape Cod

Atlantic
Ocean

EUI

In 1620, the ship *Mayflower*
carried a group of settlers from
England to what became Plymouth,
Massachusetts, one of the first
English colonies in the Americas.

AFRICA

1

Before the Bill of Rights

In the 1600s, people began fleeing Great Britain for colonies in North America. They had many different reasons. Some colonists wanted religious freedom. Others wanted a better chance to own land and make a living. There were also colonists who hoped to find or create a better, fairer system of government. When the colonists arrived in North America, the land was inhabited by thriving communities of Native Americans, the continent's first people. They had their own systems of government. Decades of conflict between Native Americans and settlers would follow as the colonies grew.

No Escape

Sometimes, British officials provided no reason when they arrested colonists.

Colonists in America still had to follow Britain's rules, and it was risky to protest against the king. If an official did not like what colonists said or wrote, they would be jailed—or worse!

Imagine you were a colonist. Soldiers and other government officials needed only a simple piece of paper to search you, your home, and all your stuff. At times, the government housed soldiers in your own bed! You would have to give them your lunch, too.

The killing of Crispus Attucks and others in the Boston Massacre convinced many colonists to reject British rule.

The Revolt

By the 1770s, many colonists wanted to end British rule. People gathered in protest. They passed out flyers announcing their complaints and spoke out in public. One demonstration in 1770 ended when British soldiers fired on the protesters. The event became known as the Boston Massacre. The soldiers killed Crispus Attucks, a man of Wampanoag and African descent, and several other colonists. Their deaths inspired more colonists to support ending British rule. Five years later, the Revolutionary War began.

The Constitution

The war lasted until 1783. Four years later, state **delegates** met in Philadelphia to draft a constitution, or set of laws. Once the document was written, three delegates refused to sign it. The document didn't list many basic rights, so it didn't protect the freedoms that colonists had fought to gain. The delegates agreed to eventually add a list of these rights, which we call the Bill of Rights. Then the Constitution was sent to the states to be **ratified**.

Only 12 of the original 13 states sent delegates to help write the Constitution. Rhode Island chose not to attend.

Balo

"A Bill of Rights? — Don't you *trust* me?"

The king in this cartoon is trying to talk his people out of having a Bill of Rights. Why? Is his argument convincing? Did the delegates who wrote the Constitution trust kings? Do you?

Inspiration for Rights

We have some severe British rulers to thank for inspiring our rights. Kings in the Middle Ages (from roughly the 5th through the 14th centuries CE) could enact cruel laws and punishments as they liked. In 1215, British noblemen forced the king to sign the Magna Carta. This agreement limited what a king could do against nobles. Then in 1689, lawmakers enacted an English Bill of Rights.

It included many familiar freedoms, such as speech. It also outlined how elected leaders could limit a ruler's power.

By signing the 1689 English Bill of Rights, British rulers Mary II and William III promised to share power with a group of lawmakers.

There were 14 original, handwritten copies of the Bill of Rights.

Bill of Rights

Congress of the United States
begun and held at the City of New York, on
Wednesday the Fourth of March, one thousand seven hundred and eighty nine

The Bill of Rights was proposed three months after the Constitution was signed.

2

Building a Nation

Imagine how relieved Americans were! They had won a war for independence and adopted fair laws and a plan to run their country. There was, however, still more to do. With the Constitution ratified, it was time for Congress to create the promised list of rights. The Constitution stated that new changes, called amendments, could be added. The first 10 **amendments** added to the Constitution would be called the Bill of Rights.

Writing the Rights

In 1789, George Washington was elected president. The U.S. Senate and House of Representatives, which together form Congress, met for the first time. James Madison, now a member of the House, reminded Congress to create a Bill of Rights. The lawmakers suggested many amendments to include in it. The House of Representatives debated and settled on 17. They sent the amendments to the Senate, which approved 12.

James Madison at first believed the individual rights granted in the Constitution were enough, but he later changed his mind. He became known as the Father of the Bill of Rights.

The 12 amendments were handwritten and delivered to each of now 14 states. Ten states needed to ratify each amendment before it could be added to the Constitution. Some states ratified all 12, while others did not ratify any. New Jersey was the first state to ratify, and it approved 11. On December 15, 1791, Virginia became the 11th and last state needed to ratify 10 of the amendments. Those amendments became the Bill of Rights.

This cartoon shows one of the delegates discussing a possible addition to the Constitution. How do the other people in the room feel about his suggestion? In your opinion, are there any mistakes in the Constitution or Bill of Rights?

SIPRESS

"Now, should we add something at the end about how wise we are and therefore nothing in here should ever be changed?"

Massachusetts, Connecticut, and Georgia did not formally approve the Bill of Rights until 1939.

ALL POWER TO THE PEOPLE

Free Expression

Witter Bynner

This mural in New Mexico was created to encourage people of diverse backgrounds to vote.

The First Four

The amendments in the Bill of Rights are so much a part of the United States today that you may wonder why the government even needed to write them down. At the time, though, these were new ideas. Many state lawmakers and the first U.S. Congress wanted things to change.

All of the freedoms in the Bill of Rights have certain limits. Most of these limits are for when someone's life or well-being is in danger.

First Amendment

Congress made sure that Americans are free to share what they think and believe, even if their ideas go against the government. The First Amendment has five powerful statements. The first specifies freedom of speech. This means that in the United States, you can voice your beliefs and complaints by speaking them aloud in public, playing music, painting a picture, acting in a play, writing a book, or marching in a protest.

Take a look at this cartoon. What do you think the creator is suggesting about the freedom of speech? Think of some times you have shared an opinion with other people. Was it difficult or easy to share? What were the consequences? Did the others agree with you?

President Donald Trump talks to a group of reporters.

People rely on the freedom of the press to hear the news.

The amendment's four other statements are also very important. You are free to believe in any religion or no religion at all. And remember those secret meetings colonists held? The First Amendment lets you **assemble** in public. It also grants freedom of the press. Newspapers, radio and television stations, and internet sites may express their ideas. Lastly, you may contact your lawmakers. Lawmakers work for you!

The Second Amendment gives citizens the right to own weapons to protect themselves and feed their families. Many today wonder if there should be limits to gun ownership.

Second Amendment

The Second Amendment states that citizens may "bear arms," or own weapons. In early America, colonists needed to hunt for food and wanted to protect themselves from thieves and other criminals. In the wilderness, people had to guard against dangerous animals. Some settlers also used weapons to seize lands from Native Americans. Finally, the delegates had not forgotten that people needed weapons when they rose up against the British government during the Revolutionary War.

Third Amendment

The Third Amendment is probably never going to affect you. Why? The amendment says the government cannot order soldiers to stay in your house. They cannot demand food, money, or a place to sleep. This was important at the time. When the states were colonies, British soldiers often invaded people's homes and took their property. The government can limit this amendment in times of war, such as the Civil War (1861–1865). You may need to house soldiers then, but the government will pay for it.

These young soldiers are proud to defend the freedoms in the Bill of Rights.

Fourth Amendment

The Fourth Amendment protects you from unreasonable search and **seizure**. Police cannot force their way into your home to search it. They can't arrest you or take away your papers or other property, either. To do any of these things, the police and other law enforcement need a good reason, or probable cause, and usually a **warrant**.

British soldiers and other officials did not always provide a good reason for arresting someone or searching their home and posessions.

Some warrants say that officers can conduct a search only during the daytime.

Unless there is an emergency or the police have another strong reason, officers need a warrant to enter a home.

A warrant is a document that gives police or other officials permission to do something. Only a judge or other court authority can approve a warrant. Police must prove to the court that there is a strong reason for a search or seizure. Then the judge issues the warrant that says exactly where the police can search or who they can arrest.

Should the First Amendment Change?

Civil rights leader Dr. Martin Luther King Jr. talks to people in New York in 1965.

The First Amendment says Congress cannot pass a law that takes away a person's right to free speech. The amendment does not include specific limits to this amendment. Today, some people argue that all speech should be free and protected. Others argue that times have changed since the Bill of Rights was written and speech should have some limits. The courts, however, have said very strongly that speech can be limited only when it is intended to or likely to cause violence.

What do you think?

Should freedom of speech be changed or limited?

YES	NO
✔ Some people spread ideas that are mean and untrue. Hate-filled speech divides people into enemy camps.	✔ People who share their ideas help inform others.
✔ Modern communication—internet, cell phones, podcasts, and television—makes it easy to spread hateful information much more quickly than when the Bill of Rights was written.	✔ Americans who are free to speak up help keep leaders from acting poorly.
✔ When some protestors express offensive opinions, they can cause a dangerous situation, such as a riot.	✔ Because the First Amendment does not specifically limit what you say, you can tell a joke, paint a picture, or write a book criticizing the government without fear of punishment.
✔ Bullying and cyberbullying are types of free speech that can cause serious harm to others. They should not be lawful.	✔ Most great changes in society happened because freedom of speech protected people like Dr. Martin Luther King Jr. (pictured here), who spoke out for important causes.

The Bill of Rights includes 16 guarantees for people accused of crimes.

Have you ever been blamed for something you did not do? What if you could not tell your side of the story? The Bill of Rights is on your side.

4

Amendments Five Through Ten

The Fifth through Eighth Amendments protect you from unfair treatment if you are accused of a crime. When Congress wrote the Bill of Rights, it was difficult, sometimes impossible, for people to defend themselves. The Ninth Amendment ensures that any right the delegates forgot to include could be added in the future. The Tenth Amendment is the only amendment in the Bill of Rights that is not about people's rights at all.

Let's take a look!

Fifth and Sixth Amendments

The Fifth Amendment has five parts:

1. You can have a grand **jury** for major crimes. A grand jury decides if there is enough evidence for a trial.

2. You cannot be tried twice for the same crime.

3. You do not have to testify against yourself. This is what it means when a person "takes the fifth."

4. You have a right to **due process**, or a fair trial.

5. The government cannot take property without paying for it.

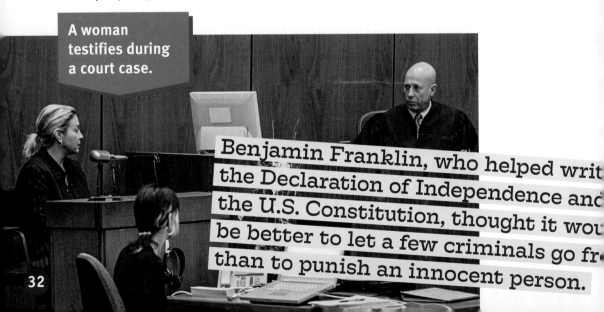

A woman testifies during a court case.

Benjamin Franklin, who helped writ[e] the Declaration of Independence and the U.S. Constitution, thought it wou[ld] be better to let a few criminals go fr[ee] than to punish an innocent person.

Citizens must report for jury duty when the court asks them to, unless they have strong reasons why they cannot.

The Sixth Amendment gives rights to accused people. It promises you a speedy and public trial, and the right to have a jury. A public trial keeps the government from having secret trials. You must know what you are being tried for, and you are allowed to see and talk to the person who accused you. You can force people to testify in your defense. You also have the right to have an attorney, even if you cannot afford one.

Seventh and Eighth Amendments

The Seventh Amendment deals with **lawsuits** between citizens. If your neighbors believe you owe them money, they can take you to court. If the amount is more than $75,000, you can have a jury trial. The amendment also states that only the government can set up a court, not you.

The Eighth Amendment says that you cannot be charged extreme fines or be forced to pay an unfairly high **bail**. You also can't be sentenced to cruel or unusual punishment.

This cartoon shows a courtroom scene, with a lawyer grilling a crack on the witness stand. What is the lawyer asking? How similar do you think this is to real testimony in court?

"So it's your testimony that you ARE NOT the crack that my client stepped on, causing him to break his back?"

Ernesto Miranda

Miranda Rights

Ernesto Miranda was arrested in 1963 for a crime in Arizona. The police forced him to confess, and he was found guilty in court. His lawyers **appealed** the verdict. They argued that police had violated Miranda's Fifth and Sixth Amendment rights. The police did not tell Miranda that he could have a lawyer with him during questioning or that he did not have to testify against himself. His case went to the Supreme Court. The court ruled that police must tell any person they arrest or question that he or she has the right to remain silent and the right to a lawyer. Today, those rights are called Miranda rights.

WARNING AS TO YOUR RIGHTS

You are under arrest. Before we ask you any questions, you must understand what your rights are.

You have the right to remain silent. You are not required to say anything to us at any time or to answer any questions. Anything you say can be used against you in court.

You have the right to talk to a lawyer for advice before we question you and to have him with you during questioning.

If you cannot afford a lawyer and want one, a lawyer will be provided for you.

If you want to answer questions now without a lawyer present you will still have the right to stop answering at any time. You also have the right to stop answering at any time until you talk to a lawyer.

P 447

The Final Two

The Ninth Amendment does not name any specific rights, but it is still very important. It protects rights that the delegates forgot or did not think to include in the Constitution or the other amendments. It means the government can't take away rights just because they aren't listed.

The Tenth Amendment protects the rights of states to have their own laws. States have different economies, populations, and geography, so their residents have different wants and needs.

Every year when I begin this unit on the Constitution, I feel I have to make it very clear that the Bill of Rights does not necessarily apply in this classroom.

Schools sometimes limit certain rights for their students. Some people argue this helps create a good learning environment. Others think it goes against the Constitution. Many believe it depends on the rule. What limits to freedom do you face in school? Why are those limits there? Do they work? Are they fair?

Women who believed in their right to vote were called suffragettes.

Left Out!

When the amendments went into effect in 1791, only white, wealthy, male landowners could vote. Lawmakers at the time considered women the property of their husbands or fathers. Enslaved African Americans were also considered to be property. Native Americans, despite being on the land first, were not recognized as citizens.

In 1870, after the Civil War (1861–1865), African American men received the right to vote. Women gained the vote across the United States in 1920. Native Americans were finally granted citizenship in 1924. However, it took four more decades for them to be granted voting rights in all 50 states.

Students in Arizona sit on the steps of their high school during a demonstration of support for victims of school shootings.

On March 14, 2018, millions of students left class to protest gun violence in the National School Walkout.

CHAPTER

5

The Bill of Rights, the Supreme Court, and You

If you feel your rights have been violated, you can take the issue to court. The Supreme Court has decided many cases that have to do with the Bill of Rights. Some directly affect students like you. One example is *West Side Community Schools v. Mergens*. In this 1990 case, the Supreme Court ruled that schools must allow religious and political student clubs if they allow other clubs that are not based on classes. This is just one example of many.

Defining Rights

In 1927 and the 1940s, members of the religious group Jehovah's Witnesses protested their schools' requirement to say the Pledge of Allegiance. The pledge was against their religion. The Supreme Court ruled in 1943 that public schools cannot force students to salute the flag or say the pledge. In 2000, families sued a school when prayers were said over a loudspeaker at football games. The Supreme Court ruled that the prayers violate freedom of religion.

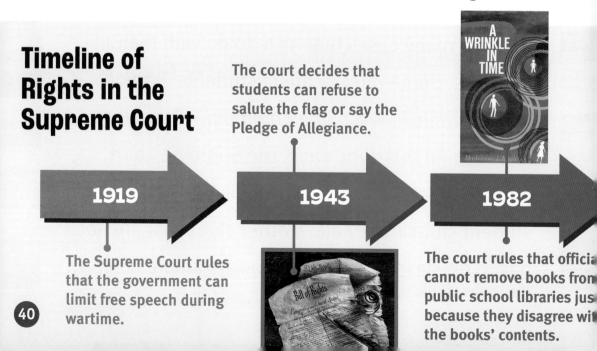

Timeline of Rights in the Supreme Court

The court decides that students can refuse to salute the flag or say the Pledge of Allegiance.

1919

1943

1982

The Supreme Court rules that the government can limit free speech during wartime.

The court rules that officia[l]s cannot remove books from public school libraries jus[t] because they disagree wi[th] the books' contents.

Looking Ahead

The writers of the Bill of Rights did not imagine today's technology. If your neighbors fly a drone over your yard, are they violating your Fourth Amendment right? If you are accused of a crime, can the police take your cell phone? Do you have to tell the police your passwords, or does the Fifth Amendment protect you? People are still debating these and other questions. Times change, but the Bill of Rights remains.

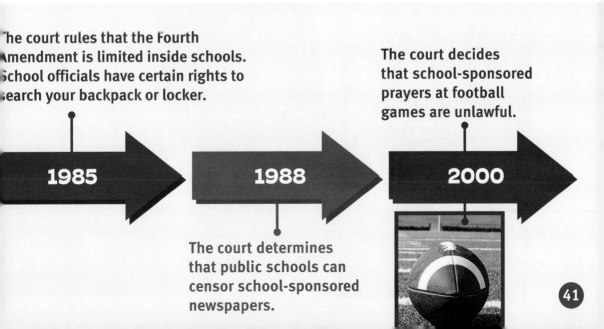

The court rules that the Fourth Amendment is limited inside schools. School officials have certain rights to search your backpack or locker.

1985

The court determines that public schools can censor school-sponsored newspapers.

1988

The court decides that school-sponsored prayers at football games are unlawful.

2000

Freedom to Read

Kids have the same power every American has to take a case to court.

All over the country, people have challenged books they disagree with. They demand that public and school libraries ban those books. Over the decades, these books have included *James and the Giant Peach*, *Harry Potter and the Sorcerer's Stone*, and *A Wrinkle in Time*. In 1976, Steven Pico was a young teen when he sued his New York school district for banning 11 books from the school library.

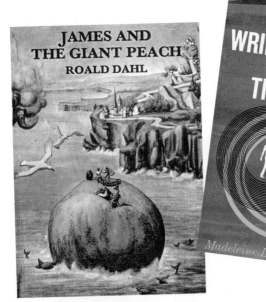

Many children's books have been challenged or banned because some people think the books will encourage witchcraft, disobedience, dishonesty, or disrespect.

Each year across the country, librarians, teachers, booksellers, and publishers protest censorship during Banned Books Week.

His case lasted six years and was finally heard by the Supreme Court. The judges sided with him. They ruled that the Bill of Rights limits the reasons a school can ban books. Students have a First Amendment right to information. Schools cannot limit the kinds of political or religious views that books present. They can only ban books when the content is vulgar or otherwise unsuitable for the students' ages.

Get Involved!

There are many things you can do to protect and support your rights. You can start by making your opinions heard. Here are a few ways you can do that:

Talk to adults around you—parents, relatives, teachers, coaches, religious leaders, or anyone else you trust.

Write a letter to your school or local newspaper.

Put together a discussion group of friends or classmates.

Write a letter or an email to your school, school board, or local government (mayor, council, commissioner, etc.).

Call, write, or email your state and national representatives in government.

Did you find the truth?

(F) Connecticut was the first state to approve the Bill of Rights.

(T) The Bill of Rights allows you to voice your beliefs by playing music.

Resources

The book you just read is a first introduction to the Bill of Rights, and to the history and government of our country. There is always more to learn and discover. In addition to this title, we encourage you to seek out complementary resources.

Other books in this series:

You can also look at:

Barcella, Laura. *Know Your Rights! A Modern Kid's Guide to the American Constitution*. New York: Sterling Children's Books, 2018.

Hoover, Stephanie. *Freedom of Religion*. New York: Gareth Stevens, 2017.

Krull, Kathleen. *A Kids' Guide to America's Bill of Rights*. New York: Harper Collins, 2015.

Micklos, John, and Richard Bell. *The First Amendment: Freedom of Speech and Religion*. Mankato, MN: Capstone Press, 2018.

Micklos, John, and Richard Bell. *The Fourth Amendment: Civil Liberties*. Mankato, MN: Capstone Press, 2018.

Glossary

amendments (uh-MEND-muhnts) changes that are made to a law or a legal document

appealed (uh-PEELD) applied to a higher court for a change in a legal decision

assemble (uh-SEM-buhl) to gather in one place

bail (BAYL) money paid to a court for the release of someone accused of a crime, with the promise that he or she will show up for the trial

delegates (DEL-uh-gits) people who represent other people in a meeting or in a legislature

due process (DOO PRAH-sess) fair treatment in trials and other aspects of the justice system

jury (JOOR-ee) a group of people, usually 12 in number, who listen to the facts at a trial and decide whether the accused person is innocent or guilty

lawsuits (LAW-soots) cases that are taken to court

ratified (RAT-uh-fyed) agreed to or approved officially

seizure (SEE-zhur) the act of seizing, or taking, something or someone

warrant (WOR-uhnt) an official piece of paper that gives someone the right to do something

Index

Page numbers in **bold** indicate illustrations.

About the Author

Ruth Bjorklund graduated from the University of Washington with a master's degree in library and information science. She has written numerous books for young people on a variety of topics, including American history, country studies, biography, wildlife, alternative energy, and the environment. Bjorklund lives with her husband and daughter on Bainbridge Island, a short ferry ride away from Seattle, Washington.